DALL-E Delights: Unleashing Creativity with AI Art for Novices

Lori H. Garcia

Published by Lori H. Garcia, 2024.

While every precaution has been taken in the preparation of this book, the publisher assumes no responsibility for errors or omissions, or for damages resulting from the use of the information contained herein.

DALL-E DELIGHTS: UNLEASHING CREATIVITY WITH AI ART FOR NOVICES

First edition. March 18, 2024.

ISBN: 979-8224063697

Written by Lori H. Garcia.

Table of Contents

Chapter 1: Introduction

What is DALL-E?

At the heart of DALL-E lies a powerful neural network that has been carefully trained on an unparalleled corpus of data with a staggering number of textual captions coupled with corresponding images. Traversing a vast realm of creativity, DALL-E paints vivid pictures, taking inspiration from a myriad of criterion, expertly capturing facets of everyday life, and expanding the realms of pure imagination.

Driven by this wealth of knowledge absorbed during its training, DALL-E holds profound capabilities to generate brand new images from scratch based solely on textual descriptions fed into its refined system. Picture this: You describe to DALL-E a freshwater lake at sunrise, adorned with towering snow-capped mountains in the backdrop, as a curious flock of flamingos dance in unison by the shimmering shores. DALL-E, ceaselessly learning, would then dare to dream with visual fidelity, synthesizing the most awe-inspiring depiction of your verbal prompt.

What elevates DALL-E beyond a mere image generator and into the realm of true artistic expression is its ability to go beyond conventional shapes, colors, and conformities. A dynamic force imbued with interpretive vision, it comprehends abstract notions, perceives elusive concepts, and creates stunning visualizations that awaken awe and astonishment within the human experience.

To master this remarkable entity, one must garner an understanding of the intricate workings that makes DALL-E tick. The internally programmed generator not only combines various datasets but showcases innate abilities to associate visual components with contextual meaning effectively—a feat that even the most visionary master painters struggle to encapsulate. Within milliseconds, DALL-E can weave its artistic prowess upon the empty canvas of our imagination, transcending limitations previously unheard of.

As a technology that effortlessly ventures into the realms of surrealism, impressionism, and every possible school of artistry, DALL-E flexes its intellectual muscles, leaving us uniquely captivated. Words and scenes transformed into vibrant compositions that taunt, tease, and intrigue the human psyche, enriching intellectual resilience as theoretical realizations transform seamlessly into imagined reality.

As awe-inspiring as it may sound, DALL-E does not come without its ethical conundrums. The composition of images entirely from scratch introduces profound questions about the artistic process and intellectual property. When does inspiration morph into replication, and where does one draw the line between imitation and originality. The burden to explore these boundaries lies at the interface between human creators and the evolving AI landscape, necessitating a delicate synergy between these two forces that embody the spirit of innovation.

In navigating the unchartered waters of creative mastery that DALL-E enables, we come face-to-face with one of humanity's most fervent aspirations: cultivating imagination, transcending limits, and painting dreams. As human curiosity intersects with technological excellence, DALL-E reveals itself to society as a muse—one that pieces together our fragmented visions and extends them even further, confounding perception, and challenging our very senses.

Harnessing the untapped potential within the realms of artificial intelligence, DALL-E illuminates endless possibilities for collaboration between humans and computer-generated creativity. The virtuosity of DALL-E unfolds beyond the realm of visual aesthetics, manifesting a world where brilliance is rooted in the fusion of collective imagination and cutting-edge technology. Shall we step into this immersive domain and embark on an awe-inspiring journey of artistry, bridging the gap between humanity and machine, where imagination knows no bounds.

Purpose of this Guide

DALL-E gets its name from a clever combination of the renowned Spanish painter, Salvador Dalí, who is known for his surreal and imaginative creations, and Pixar's adorable character WALL-E. These iconic symbols represent the two fundamental elements intrinsic to DALL-E: creativity and visual representation. DALL-E takes written descriptions as input and produces stunning, sometimes bizarre, images as output. As we delve further into this guide, you will witness how DALL-E can bring your wildest, most imaginative ideas to life through its intricate algorithms and extraordinary capabilities.

Understanding how DALL-E operates will aid us in comprehending the breadth of its artistic prowess. To create this astounding AI, OpenAI employed a technique known as unsupervised learning, transforming a staggering dataset of diverse images into a vast amount of small puzzle pieces. These pieces, referred to as "tokens," help DALL-E navigate the complexity of generating accurate and meaningful images based on the textual prompts it receives.

Tokens form a fundamental building block in the architecture of DALL-E. For our purposes, each prompt, or textual description, we feed into DALL-E is encoded into a series of tokens that facilitate the model's understanding of our creative intentions. These tokens act as interactive triggers for DALL-E, allowing it to unravel their meaning and subsequently generate visuals accordingly. Understanding the interplay of tokens and DALL-E's internal processes enables us to maximize the creative potential of this remarkable AI model.

However, like any technological breakthrough, DALL-E also has its limitations. While it can generate vivid and highly original imagery, it may sometimes struggle with specific requests or produce unexpected results. Additionally, its abilities are shaped entirely by the data it has been trained on, which means that it may lack real-world knowledge or exhibit biases present in the training dataset. Keeping these limitations in mind is crucial as we traverse the realm of DALL-E, striking a careful balance between relying on its immense creative capabilities and maintaining a nuanced awareness of its boundaries.

As we venture forth into this guide, be prepared to unleash the power of DALL-E for your creative pursuits. From creating whimsical characters to picturing exotic landscapes, envisioning futuristic objects to illustrating intangible concepts, DALL-E will serve as your faithful companion – always at the ready to breathe visual life into your ideas. Through a series of tutorials, tips, and artistic examples, you will unlock the immense potential of this ground-breaking AI, surprising yourself with the boundless artistic feats you can achieve with DALL-E.

So, dear reader, fasten your seatbelts, for an epic journey into the realm of DALL-E is about to commence. Prepare to witness the previously unimaginable, to experience the collision of imagination with artificial intelligence, and to embark on a quest to realize your wildest creative dreams. With this guide in hand, you will acquire the knowledge and skills required to wield DALL-E with confidence, becoming a true artist in the realm of AI. Together, let us unlock the extraordinary potential of DALL-E and explore the uncharted territories of our artistic minds.

Chapter 2: Getting Started

Creating an Account

Accessing DALL-E Interface

To embark on a journey of accessing the DALL-E interface and fully utilize this groundbreaking AI tool, it is essential to understand the underlying technology and its workings. DALL-E relies on a two-step process to generate images based on textual prompts provided by a user. First, the model repurposes pre-existing images from its vast dataset by using similarities within the given text. Then, it engages in a delicate process of image composition, transforming existing images or creating entirely new ones tailored to the supplied description.

Now, let us delve into the intricacies of accessing the DALL-E interface. To begin your exploration, you will need an internet-connected device such as a computer or smartphone. Accessing the interface can be accomplished by navigating to the OpenAI website, where you will find the DALL-E application effortlessly integrated within their user-friendly platform. Once there, you will be greeted by an intuitive and visually appealing interface that beckons you to unlock your creative potential.

To enter the world of imagination and creativity that DALL-E affords, you can simply compose a textual description that conveys your desired image. It is imperative to be as clear and detailed as possible, painting a vivid picture with your words. Whether you aim to depict a fantastical creature, an awe-inspiring landscape, or an abstract concept, DALL-E can transform your vision into a striking visual representation.

Interacting with the DALL-E interface is a seamless experience that ensures even novice users feel at ease. Once you have composed your textual prompt, the interface presents you with the generated image, fulfilling your creative vision or redefining it into something unexpected and tremendous. DALL-E also grants users the option to modify and fine-tune the generated image by utilizing sliders to adjust various parameters, such as color, perspective, and size. This adaptive feature allows users to explore different possibilities and tailor the image precisely to their liking.

Beyond the interactive capabilities of the DALL-E interface, it is essential to recognize the potential applications and implications that this technology carries. From aiding artists in conceptualizing their ideas and providing fresh perspectives, to revolutionizing the advertising and design industries, DALL-E's impact is far-reaching. Its ability to generate high-quality, unique images based on textual descriptions has captured the imaginations of professionals and enthusiasts alike. However, it is crucial to approach DALL-E and other AI models with an ethical awareness, understanding the profound responsibility that accompanies their use in shaping the world of visual creativity.

As you embark on your journey with DALL-E and immerse yourself in its remarkable potential, remember to embrace the creative power this AI model unlocks. Allow the synergy of your imagination and the advanced capabilities of DALL-E to guide you in harnessing newfound realms of expression and innovation.

Chapter 3: Basic Functions

Image Generation Basics

Understanding Inputs

DALL-E's inception marks an unparalleled leap in the realm of machine learning. Originally an extension of the infamous GPT-3, DALL-E boasts an architecture designed to interpret inputs and construct seemingly limitless visual creations with its immense creative language. This revolutionary neural network model draws upon an impressive dataset curated from various online imagery. This dataset comprises an astonishing 12 billion images, selected to expose DALL-E to the extensive nuances and intricacies present within the visual world.

To better understand the functioning of this extraordinary AI, let us delve into its inner workings. Behind DALL-E's phenomenal capabilities lies its two integral components: the generator and the discriminator. The generator aims to produce realistic images that fit a given textual description, while the discriminator serves as a discerning metric to critique and improve the quality of these generated images. Through an iterative training process, these components steadily become more proficient and sophisticated, ultimately allowing DALL-E to create exceptional visuals akin to those produced by the human imagination.

Despite the seemingly limitless possibilities DALL-E portrays, it is important to recognize that the extensive training does not equal explicit knowledge. While it may seem contradictory, DALL-E's understanding of visual stimuli can be equated to learning patterns without a grasp of the content. It cannot actively comprehend the intricate details of an image or provide relevant details that aren't inherent in the training dataset.

Nonetheless, the astounding creativity and aesthetic prowess offered by DALL-E's output are formidable. From generating fantastical creatures like fire-breathing snails to rendering everyday objects with curious modifications, DALL-E's ability to create art has captivated individuals and industries alike. Artists, designers, and writers swiftly embraced this technology as a powerful tool for realizing their wildest ideas.

However, utilizing DALL-E effectively requires a nuanced understanding of its inputs. This understanding facilitates improving the quality of generated images and ensures the compatibility of the textual prompts provided. The interactive imagination between 'text' and 'images' becomes an important foundation for executing DALL-E's potential to the fullest extent.

To comprehend the input requirements for DALL-E, a crucial aspect to consider is feature dependency. Remarkably, minor modifications to the textual description can leave significant impacts on the output image. Changing a single word or attempting a slightly different narrative might generate vastly distinct visual outcomes. As users, we need to convey our intentions with precise wording and deliberate phrasing to get the desired results. The level of clarity and specificity supplied within the textual prompt serves as a crucial guide for DALL-E in shaping its output.

In conclusion, the possibilities presented by DALL-E are awe-inspiring. Unlocking the true potential of this miraculous AI model requires a deep understanding of its underlying mechanisms, as well as astutely crafting textual prompts for generating specific imagery. As the worlds of art, design, and technology increasingly intertwine, DALL-E truly stands at the forefront, providing a path to harnessing the boundless creative capabilities of machine learning. One can only marvel at the possibilities that await as we continue to explore and develop the extraordinary power of DALL-E.

Chapter 4: Advanced Features

Exploring Advanced Options

When OpenAI unveiled its revolutionary text-to-image generator, DALL-E, the world of artificial intelligence experienced a paradigm shift. DALL-E's ability to create unique and imaginative visual outputs based on textual prompts sparked immense fascination and promised limitless creative possibilities. Within the context of this chapter, we embark on an exciting journey to explore DALL-E's advanced options and arm ourselves with the knowledge to fully harness its novel capabilities.

Section 1: Transcending Limitations: Synthesizing Abstract Concepts

1. 1 Mapping Abstract Ideas to DALL-E Inputs

While DALL-E exhibits an impressive ability to generate images of concrete objects, we often find ourselves intrigued by the challenge of visualizing abstract concepts. Within the context of this section, we delve into techniques that allow us to bridge the gap between conceptualizing abstract ideas and using DALL-E's vast dataset.

1. 2 Crafting Textual Prompts: Nurturing the Abstract

Crafting textual prompts can be an art form in itself. To explore DALL-E's potential to generate abstract imagery, we learn to optimize our prompts by employing imaginative descriptions, evocative metaphors, and cross-domain interactions. Unearthing DALL-E's latent ability to depict concepts and emotions through its seemingly endless repertoire takes our creative powers to new heights.

Section 2: Behind the Scenes: Training Data and Neuron-Level Fine-Tuning

2. 1 Investigating DALL-E's Training Data: Enriching Imagery References

Understanding the neural network's training is crucial to comprehend how DALL-E generates diverse outputs. We shed light on the origins of DALL-E's training data, examining the processes that blend a myriad of images into the knowledge it operates on. This knowledge assists us in shaping our expectations and fueling our creative tasks.

2. 2 Neuron-Level Fine-Tuning: Expanding Controls

While beloved for its autonomous creativity, DALL-E also grants users an opportunity to exert control over its output. We explore the potential of fine-tuning its neurons, enabling us to impose our artistic preferences to an unprecedented level. By modifying specific contextual information, we unleash a diverse array of creative techniques that take DALL-E's creativity to unexplored realms.

Section 3: Practical Transformation: Refining Output Characteristics

3. 1 Style Transfer and Image Stylization: Blending Visual Languages

By embracing the principles of style transfer and image stylization, we discover techniques to manipulate DALL-E's output with unique visual signatures. Exploring multiple artistic styles and catering to various visual preferences becomes an exciting endeavor as we guide the AI model along the paths of serenity, abstraction, impressionism, or any aesthetic inclination we choose.

3. 2 Augmenting Outputs: Novel Compositions and Variations

To augment the variety of our generated images, we delve into techniques that help us use DALL-E not merely as a standalone generator but as part of a creative process. By exploring iterative design, morphological evolution, or interactive driven outputs, we discover transformative possibilities that astound us with their infinite permutations and combinations.

Conclusion: A Journey to Creative Discovery with DALL-E

As we bring this chapter to a close, we reflect on the awe-inspiring exploration we had with DALL-E's advanced options. From synthesizing abstract concepts to understanding its neural processes, and transforming outputs based on preferred styles, we embarked on an exhilarating journey of self-expression. The unlimited potential of DALL-E becomes clear as we leverage its capabilities, not just to generate visual imagery, but to foster our creativity, inspire innovation, and provide a canvas for human-artificial symbiosis that helps us transcend boundaries never dreamt of before.

Customizing Outputs

D ALL-E is an AI system that generates unique images from textual prompts, essentially providing a bridge between words and visual content. Amid this chapter, you will learn step-by-step how to leverage DALL-E's capabilities to tailor outputs to meet your creative vision and language inputs.

1. Understanding Prompt Customization:

Customizing the outputs of DALL-E begins with crafting the right prompts. It is crucial to provide clear and specific instructions to the model to receive the desired results. Whether you want a melting clock or a fantastical landscape, clarity is key. Be precise in language choice and vividly describe the details you wish to see in the generated image.

2. Exploring Size and Resolution:

DALL-E lets you control both the size and resolution of the output images. You can specify your preferred dimensions, aspect ratio, and resolution to ensure the generated images meet your requirements. Whether you need high-quality print-ready images or images optimized for the web, DALL-E empowers you with the tools to design to these specifications.

3. Navigating Creative Constraints:

While DALL-E can create an astounding range of images, it is essential to bear in mind the limitations of the model. Experimentation is key to discovering the boundaries. For instance, intricate details or specific poses may be challenging for the model to replicate accurately. Understanding these minor constraints will enable you to fine-tune your prompts and align expectations.

4. Exploring Appearance Details:

DALL-E not only generates images that show objects but also provides control over their appearances, allowing you to iterate within your prompt to yield a desirable outcome. Whether you want a yellow sun or a meandering river, DALL-E's impressive training equips it to manipulate attributes like color, shape, texture, and style to generate images that match your vision.

5. Manipulating Semantic Meaning:

In addition to appearance, DALL-E can manipulate semantic meanings based on your directions. For example, specifying instructions such as "a tree made of clouds" or "a city underwater" challenges the system to create imaginative compositions. Experimenting with different linguistic phrases and metaphorical descriptions offers endless possibilities for unique outputs.

6. Iterating and Contextualizing:

Don't be afraid to experiment! The true power of DALL-E lies in its ability to refine outputs over multiple iterations. You can tweak your prompts, refine your language, and combine inputs to achieve the desired result. Exploring various narrative styles, moods, or stylistic references encourages creativity and diversity in the generated images.

7. Balancing Novelty and Realism:

Harnessing the remarkable generative capabilities of DALL-E often means balancing novelty with realism to achieve compelling images. While unusual compositions may appeal in certain scenarios, blending elements in a way that retains the essence of natural photographs can lend a more immersive and visually engrossing experience to the generated outputs.

Developing proficiency in customizing DALL-E outputs requires not just an understanding of its capabilities but also an appreciation for creative experimentation. Through practice and exploration, you will discover unique ways to express your ideas by bridging your imagination with DALL-E's vast neural network.

So, prepare to let your imagination soar as you further explore the remarkable depths of DALL-E's adaptations and embrace the infinite possibilities it offers for image generation and customization to bring your wildest concepts and fancies to life.

Chapter 5: Using DALL-E Effectively

Tips for Efficient Usage

1. Understand the Capabilities of DALL-E:
Before diving into using DALL-E, it is crucial to familiarize yourself with its capabilities and limitations. This knowledge will lay the foundation for your successful usage and enable you to explore and exploit the model to its fullest potential. Begin by educating yourself about DALL-E's training methodology, its reliance on Transformer models, and concepts like neural networks and generative models.

2. Craft Specific Prompts:
To obtain the desired output from DALL-E, it is important to provide clear and specific prompts. For instance, instead of relying on broad descriptions like "yellow flower," you can specify the type of flower you desire, such as "tulip," "sunflower," or "daisy." Adding relevant adjectives or attributes like "bright yellow tulip" will further enhance the specificity of your prompt, allowing DALL-E to generate a more accurate image.

3. Leverage Conceptual Blends:
Conceptual blending is a cognitive process that combines different concepts to create new ideas. Similarly, in using DALL-E, you can experiment with blending different concepts within a single prompt, resulting in fascinating and creative outputs. For instance, prompt DALL-E with "an elephant with butterfly wings," giving the model two distinct concepts to merge, which can lead to surprising and delightful results.

4. Utilize Conditional Prompts:
One of the powerful features of DALL-E is its ability to generate images based on specific conditions imposed in the prompt. For instance, you can instruct DALL-E to produce images of "a snowy landscape at night" or "different species of birds in autumn." Adding conditions and context to your prompts will help steer DALL-E's focus and generate targeted outputs.

5. Control Outputs using Prompts:

Within the prompts you provide, you can also control various aspects of the generated images, such as their color, pose, perspective, or composition. By manipulating these variables in your prompt, you can guide DALL-E to create images that adhere more closely to your vision. For example, using phrases like "a red car from a front-view perspective" or "a mug with a handle on the left side" can influence the visual output accordingly.

6. Experiment with Image Resolution and Aspect Ratio:

DALL-E allows users to specify the output image's resolution and aspect ratio by simply mentioning them in the prompts. For instance, you can request high-resolution images by prompt such as "a beach landscape in 4K resolution." Moreover, if you desire a specific aspect ratio, like a square image, include that parameter in your prompt. Such control over image properties adds further precision and flexibility to your usage of DALL-E.

7. Iterative Prompt Refinement:

In cases where the initial output does not meet your expectations or requirements, consider refining your prompts iteratively. You can do this by incrementally modifying the prompt until you achieve the desired output. Analyze the generated images, assess what aspects need improvement, and revise and iterate your prompts accordingly. This iterative process will allow you to finely tune the outputs of DALL-E.

8. Explore the Implementation of Constraints:

DALL-E allows for the inclusion of constraints in prompts to further guide the image generation process. These constraints can enforce specific features, components, or properties in the generated images. For example, you can request a prompt to limit the color palette of the image to black and white, or to possess a certain pattern or texture. Experimenting with various constraints will widen the range of creative possibilities with DALL-E.

Conclusion:

Mastering the art of efficient DALL-E usage requires a deep understanding of its capabilities, crafting specific prompts, leveraging conceptual blends, exploiting conditional prompts, controlling outputs, experimenting with resolution and aspect ratio, applying iterative prompt refinement, and exploring constraint implementation. By embracing these tips and strategies, you will be able to unlock the true power of DALL-E and enjoy an engaging and productive creative journey in the world of AI-generated visuals.

Maximizing Output Quality

The concept of creating artistic masterpieces has long been associated with human creativity. However, there has been a surprising development in the field of artificial intelligence (AI) with the emergence of models that can generate highly impressive and original images. Among these models, OpenAI's neural network, DALL-E, has proven to be a major breakthrough in the realm of creative AI. Amidst these chapter, we will delve into the complexities of learning and utilizing DALL-E - understanding its inner workings, training it effectively, and ultimately harnessing its power to maximize output quality.

Understanding DALL-E: First Steps

Before we embark upon using DALL-E, it is crucial to understand the foundations of its architecture. DALL-E operates by employing a trained neural network that generates images based on given inputs. What sets DALL-E apart is its remarkable ability to generate visually appealing and surprisingly unique images from even the most abstract textual descriptions. Furthermore, DALL-E is based on a generative language model, allowing it to generate images independently by interpreting and transforming textual prompts into visual outputs.

Training DALL-E:

To effectively employ DALL-E, one must understand the vital aspect of training the model. A well-trained and optimized DALL-E can yield remarkably high-quality results. The training process involves feeding the model with vast amounts of data, which it uses to develop an innate understanding of various visual and semantic concepts. Furthermore, by providing a diverse training dataset with a wide range of visual motifs, styles, and variations, we can enhance DALL-E's capacity to explore unique and creative outcomes.

Maximizing Output Quality:

1. Improving Exploration Efficiency:

When aiming to maximize the output quality of DALL-E, it is essential to expand the exploration space by enhancing the textual prompts. By empowering

DALL-E with more descriptive or complex inputs, such as contextual dependencies or subtleties in the composition of images, we push it beyond mere imitation and towards more inventive creations.

2. Building a Control Mechanism:

To excel in harnessing DALL-E's full capabilities, implementing a control mechanism becomes indispensable. By meticulously controlling various parameters like style, color composition, mood, or desired content, one can guide DALL-E towards generating outputs adhering to specific aesthetic aspirations. This control mechanism leverages defined prompts to instruct DALL-E, ensuring the desired output quality and compatibility with the intended purpose.

3. Leveraging Metadata and Domain-Specific Inputs:

Utilizing metadata or domain-specific information plays a pivotal role in refining DALL-E's output quality. By accommodating supplementary data, such as image tags, user preferences, or ontological knowledge, DALL-E gains insights to generate more coherent, intuitive, and visually compelling results aligned with the intended context.

4. Leveraging Fine-Tuning Techniques:

Enhancing an already-trained DALL-E by employing fine-tuning techniques becomes particularly beneficial in various use cases. Fine-tuning allows us to adapt DALL-E to perform in specific domains or cater to unique requirements, raising the level of output quality by training the model further to suit particular objectives.

5. Iterative Feedback and Validation:

Maximizing output quality necessitates an iterative approach. Continuous iterations with feedback loops, user validation, and rigorous evaluation become invaluable in the quest for continuous improvement. By incorporating qualitative and quantitative feedback, we can fine-tune DALL-E, realigning it with the vision of maximizing output quality and ensuring its full potential is effectively utilized.

Conclusion:

DALL-E represents a giant leap in AI-driven creativity, enabling humans to explore artistic possibilities otherwise inaccessible to us. Through an understanding of its architecture, effective training, and considered utilization, DALL-E's capabilities can be unlocked for maximum output quality. By embracing the concepts outlined in this chapter, we harness the full potential of DALL-E, transcending mere algorithmic generation and fostering a harmony between human creativity and the AI marvel, ultimately unlocking entirely new realms of visual imagination.

Chapter 6: Creative Applications

Generating Creative Content

Within the confines of its digital confines lay an extraordinary ability to generate limitless creative content in the form of unique images stretching the limits of the imaginings of humankind. It was an open invitation for computer programs to explore the far reaches of their artistic capabilities, a revolution that would forever redefine the boundaries of creativity itself.

Conceptualized and developed by OpenAI, DALL-E fused the potentials of deep learning and generative adversarial networks to become an unparalleled imagination machine. Trained on an imposing dataset of textual descriptions and corresponding images, DALL-E quickly learned to decipher the intricate connections between syntax, semantics, and visual perceptions. This enabled it to propose and generate novel and artistic imagery from combinational understandings not yet explored by human minds.

In essence, DALL-E allowed people to channel their vision, thoughts, and ideas directly into the virtual world. All it required was a spark of inspiration and an encoded language, and DALL-E would breathe life into a creation that had hitherto resided only in the recesses of human cognition.

To wield the potential of DALL-E, one must delve into the techniques that encapsulate its prowess. Understanding DALL-E's inner workings begins by comprehending its core components: the adversarial autoencoder.

Within this intricate architecture lies the principal force empowering DALL-E's generative aptitude. The autoencoder is comprised of two linked networks: the encoder and the decoder. The encoder unity performs the crucial task of parsing input images into a lower-dimensional feature representation, effectively extracting pivotal elements hidden within visual artifacts. Simultaneously, the decoder aspect emerges, ressembling DALL-E's artistic arm, creates kaleidoscopic visualizations based on those compressed representations retrieved from the encoder network, reconstructing reality in unforeseen ways.

To transform still imagery into a stunning illustration, DALL-E merges its reinforcement and generative paradigms in a potent synthesis encapsulated by generative adversarial networks (GANs). This amalgamation imbues DALL-E with an exquisite capability to interpret textual prompts and generate vibrant visualizations that reverberate with artistic flair.

Despite DALL-E's astounding capabilities, the process of generating content goes beyond feeding mere descriptions into the network. Artistry emanates from inquiry and exploration. Thus, the successful utilization of DALL-E relies on mastering the art of question-based interaction.

By harnessing the strength of thoughtful questioning, users can unlock the depths of DALL-E's hidden capacity. Each sentence becomes an artistic call to arms, sparking dialogues with the machine's intricate neural network and empowering it to transcend expectations. Within this dance of cognition and computation, users elaborate on seemingly incompatible concepts, weaving narratives where improbable images spring to life.

From the fusion of simple sentence prompts and the mysterious algorithms rumbling behind DALL-E's circuitry, one can summon images rooted in fantasy and realism. Hidden in its reservoir of learned embeddings, DALL-E finds the intersections between darkness and light, traditional and avant-garde, caricature and realism, teasing out illustrations once held only within the chambers of human imagination.

Be warned, however, for with great creative power comes ethical responsibility. DALL-E may unravel bold expressions, but it is up to humans to judiciously perceive, evaluate, and shepherd those creations forth. Replete with pigmentary explorations, mythical creature amalgamations, and playful surrealism, DALL-E liberates our sense of artistic possibility, but demands calibration to form a philosophical partnership dedicated to harnessing its power judiciously.

Within this chapter, we will immerse ourselves in the extraordinary universe of DALL-E, exploring its infinite potential and the role each stubborn pixel designates in becoming a bewitching artwork born from the heart of computation and the utopian infinities of human imagination. Embrace curiosity as we venture forth, bringing DALL-E alive by the instruction of words, to comprehend the enigmatic interplay uniting creative wildlands and machine intelligence.

Artistic Expressions with DALL-E

Creativity is a remarkable facet of human intelligence, capable of producing awe-inspiring and thought-provoking artistic expressions. Throughout history, art in its various forms has captivated audiences and allowed artists to convey emotions, ideas, and stories. But what if we could augment our artistic abilities and collaborate with a creative AI? Thanks to DALL-E, the groundbreaking deep-learning model developed by OpenAI, we enter a new era of artistic possibilities unlike anything we have witnessed before.

Embraced by this chapter, we will explore the world of DALL-E—an AI artist that can generate stunning, never-before-seen images from textual prompts by applying its deep knowledge of existing artworks. Beyond its immense capabilities for creating visually pleasing art, DALL-E challenges traditional boundaries with its ability to spark creativity and allow humans to engage in unprecedented artistic collaborations.

Chapter 24: Discovering DALL-E's Creation Process

Let us take a journey into the inner workings of DALL-E and understand how it brings our artistic visions to life. The core principle behind DALL-E lies in its ingenious use of a generative adversarial network (GAN), a framework that leverages both a generator and a discriminator. The generator synthesizes images from scratch based on prompt text, while the discriminator endeavors to differentiate these computer-generated images from real ones. Through an iterative process of training and refinement, DALL-E learns to generate hyper-realistic images that align with the input prompts, emphasizing diverse artistic styles and intricate details.

Chapter 25: Collaborating with DALL-E

DALL-E shines not just as an autonomous creator but also as an invaluable partner and collaborator for artists. By feeding it with conceptually rich prompts, one can stimulate DALL-E's artistic cognition, ushering in an innovative artistic synergy between humans and machines. Imagine a painter describing a dreamlike forest teeming with vibrant colors and mystical creatures, and DALL-E transforming that visualization into an otherworldly masterpiece. This creative collaboration allows artists to genuinely explore new artistic avenues without limit.

Chapter 26: Exploring Limitless Possibilities

One of DALL-E's most incredible features is its ability to push artistic boundaries and ignite our imagination. By providing prompts that lie beyond the realm of traditional art, we can activate DALL-E's creative potential and venture into uncharted artistic territories. Imagine a poet describing a surreal, intergalactic ballet of stars, and DALL-E encapsulating that vision in a celestial artwork. The resulting blend of human and AI creativity evokes profound emotions and opens up entirely new avenues for self-expression.

Chapter 27: Ethical Considerations and Responsibility

While DALL-E's artistic prowess astonishes many, it is imperative that we never lose sight of the ethical implications that come with wielding such power. As artists, it becomes our responsibility to ensure that AI creations are used appropriately and ethically. DALL-E may break new artistic ground, but it is our duty to ensure that it does not undermine the originality and hard work of human artists. Together, artists and AI must navigate an ethical framework that respects both the boundaries of inspiration and the rights of creators.

Conclusion:

DALL-E has blurred the distinction between human and machine creativity, merging the imaginative possibilities of AI with the human spirit. It challenges traditional artistic norms and emboldens creators to explore uncharted territories. As artists, we must embrace this transformative technology responsibly, ensuring that we leverage it to enhance our expression rather than diminish our authenticity. With the advent of DALL-E, the world of art is poised for a revolution, where AI and human creativity converge to unlock an era of unbounded artistic expression. Let us forge a path hand-in-hand with our AI companions, creating art that will captivate and engage audiences for generations to come.

Chapter 7: Integration

Integrating DALL-E with Other Tools

Additionally, integration with graphic design software can enable dynamic collaboration between DALL-E and designers. Design teams can leverage the AI's ability to rapidly produce a wide range of image options, allowing them to explore multiple design directions quickly. By integrating DALL-E into their existing software, designers can seamlessly incorporate the generated images into their compositions, enhancing their creative process and ultimately producing high-quality designs.

Another application lies in content creation for social media and advertising. Marketers often face challenges in sourcing or creating engaging visual content that aligns with their brand messaging. With DALL-E integration, they can now generate unique and attention-grabbing images that not only embody their brand identity but also resonate with their target audience. By feeding DALL-E with specific keywords or descriptions, marketers can receive a variety of visuals tailored to their needs, making their social media posts and advertisements more visually appealing and memorable.

Furthermore, integration with video editing software can revolutionize the way filmmakers and content creators approach their projects. DALL-E can be utilized to generate storyboards or concept art, empowering creators to visualize and experiment with scenes before committing resources to actual production. The AI's ability to swiftly generate custom visuals based on textual cues provides filmmakers with opportunities for ideation and exploration, enabling them to push creative boundaries.

Moreover, It is not just creative tools that can benefit from integrating with DALL-E; other AI models and products can also create a powerful synergy by leveraging its image generation capabilities. For example, consider the integration of DALL-E with virtual reality (VR) applications. By combining the rich visual output of DALL-E with the immersive experience of VR, developers can offer users a truly captivating and lifelike virtual environment. Whether it is generating realistic textures, characters, or landscapes, DALL-E's integration into VR technology ensures an unparalleled level of visual fidelity and immersion.

To integrate DALL-E with other tools, developers and designers can create APIs or software development kits (SDKs) that allow seamless communication between applications, enabling easy sharing of data and facilitating the incorporation of DALL-E's image generation capabilities into existing workflows. By adopting an open approach, the integration process becomes more accessible, empowering a diverse range of professionals to leverage DALL-E's potential in their respective domains.

In conclusion, the integration of DALL-E with other tools has immense potential to transform various industries. Whether it is supporting graphic designers with image generation, enhancing marketers' content creation efforts, empowering filmmakers with pre-production visualization, or revolutionizing the way VR applications immerse users, the possibilities are endless. By harnessing DALL-E's capabilities and seamlessly integrating it with existing tools, professionals can elevate their creative outputs, improve productivity, and explore new horizons of innovation.

API Integration

8. 2 The Rise of DALL-E and its Potential Applications

Upon its release, DALL-E garnered widespread attention and interest owing to its impressive power of creative image generation. The AI community, illustrators, and designers immediately recognized the revolutionary potential of this breakthrough model. For instance, despite being trained on a dataset of human-created images, DALL-E is proficient in generating entirely new, yet realistic images that possess intricate textures, shapes, and colors. This evolutionary aspect of DALL-E enables users to obtain striking visuals by stating only textual descriptions, igniting a wave of innovation across industries.

8. 3 Integration of DALL-E into an API

With its profound capabilities, DALL-E was soon made available through an application programming interface (API), enabling users to seamlessly integrate its immense creative potential into their own applications and services. Integration of DALL-E into an API forms a crucial bridge between the model and its users, offering a streamlined pathway to leverage its unparalleled image generation capabilities.

8. 4 Experimenting with DALL-E's API Integration

To make the most of DALL-E's API integration, developers are encouraged to embrace the art of experimentation and exploration. The API provides a wide range of parameters that can be adjusted to achieve desired image outputs. These parameters could include factors such as image size, image style, texture, and even rare combinations of objects. By iteratively modifying these parameters and considering the varying outcomes, developers can unlock endless possibilities within DALL-E's creative realm.

8. 5 DALL-E as a Design Asset

Design is an area where DALL-E thrives, for its ability to generate vivid visuals simply from text inputs offers designers an inexhaustible resource of inspiration. By leveraging the DALL-E API, designers can effortlessly translate their conceptual ideas into highly sophisticated visual representations. For instance, intricate patterns, unique shapes, and specific details can be described in text and realized as awe-inspiring images through the API's integration.

8. 6 Leveraging DALL-E in Artistic Expression

Beyond design, DALL-E has also proven to be a groundbreaking tool for artists seeking new forms of creative expression. By providing textual descriptions of abstract concepts or visual aesthetics, artists can generate images that capture their imagination like never before. This enables artists to explore uncharted territories and experiment with different artistic styles, pushing creative boundaries to astounding levels.

8. 7 Ethical Considerations and Responsible Usage

While DALL-E's API integration empowers users with immense creative possibilities, it is vital to consider the ethical implications of its usage. Responsible access to such a resource demands mindful usage and careful consideration of potential limitations and biases embedded in the model. Striving for transparency and actively mitigating any adverse impact on individuals or communities is pivotal for ensuring the responsible use of DALL-E and similar AI technologies.

8. 8 Conclusion: DALL-E Revolutionizing Creativity

With the integration of DALL-E into an API, its unprecedented image generation capabilities are now at the fingertips of developers, designers, and artists. This revolutionary tool has opened up a universe of creative possibilities that were unimaginable before. As we embark on this journey, it is important to embrace responsible utilization, while pushing the boundaries of creativity and innovation with DALL-E. Through exploration, experimentation, and mindful adoption, DALL-E can inspire a new era of artistic expression, design thinking, and overall technological advancement.

Chapter 8: Ethical Considerations

Ethics in AI Art

N amed in honor of the fusion of Salvador Dali and WALL-E, DALL-E is the brainchild of OpenAI, an organization striving to ensure that AI benefits all of humanity. Developed as a language-guided image generation model, DALL-E utilizes a combination of supervised training and unsupervised learning to comprehend any prompt given to it. For example, upon receiving a human-generated, textual description like "a sleepy sunflower sitting on a couch watching TV," DALL-E can generate an extraordinary and visually compelling image encapsulating that description.

With its unique capacity for transmuting textual input into vivid visual representations, DALL-E holds immense potential for transforming the way art is conceptualized and produced. It equips artists, creators, and designers with a novel tool in their creative arsenal, enabling them to visualize ideas even before they are realized on canvas or screen. However, while AI-generated art may serve as a stepping stone to unparalleled innovation, the ethical implications that emerge from technologies like DALL-E cannot be overlooked.

One of the central ethical concerns surrounding DALL-E lies in issues of authorship and intellectual property. When an AI model like DALL-E generates artwork, determining ownership becomes a complex affair. If a piece of AI art were to become highly sought after or valuable, who would be considered the creator: the AI system itself, the human who prompts the AI, the organization that developed the AI, or a combination thereof? Moreover, if an AI model learns from the copyrighted works of an artist as part of its training data, does the AI-generated artwork infringe upon copyright laws? The intersection of art and AI raises numerous questions that push the boundaries of the law and call for revised guidelines on intellectual property and attribution.

Another ethical aspect to consider pertains to the potential reinforcement or exacerbation of existing biases within AI art. In training a generative model like DALL-E, the data used plays a fundamental role in decision-making. If the training data disproportionately represents specific populations or exhibits underlying biases, there is a risk that these biases will be perpetuated in the generated imagery. This means that if integrated carelessly into AI art creation, DALL-E and similar models could inadvertently reinforce stereotypes, prejudice, or underrepresentation. It becomes imperative for designers and developers to carefully curate unbiased and diverse data to minimize potential harm and uphold ethical standards.

Furthermore, the incorporation of AI technology in art begs questions of appropriation and cultural sensitivity. With diverse cultural inheritances deeply embedded in artistic expression, AI-generated art warrants extensive analysis to discern whether it respects and pays homage to its numerous origins. The cultural context of various elements within a piece of AI art must be considered so as to prevent the appropriation of knowledge, stories, and aesthetics from marginalized communities. Adequate cultural awareness, representation, and considerations must be practiced to ensure AI art remains an instrument of respect and inclusivity.

To address these ethical concerns, responsible principles should be embedded within the design and training of AI art models like DALL-E. Organizations and researchers must promote transparency, enabling scrutiny of the underlying decision-making processes of these models. Additionally, diverse and fair training datasets, firmly rooted in the principles of inclusivity and equity, must be employed to ensure AI art does not perpetuate or amplify existing societal biases. As this field continues to evolve, collaboration between experts in AI, ethics, and art becomes vital for finding a harmonious balance between the immense creative potential of AI systems like DALL-E, and the fundamental principles of morality and social responsibility.

Responsible Usage Guidelines

P art 1: Unveiling the Marvel That is DALL-E
Nestled at the intersection of artificial intelligence and creativity, DALL-E has proven to be one of the most groundbreaking technologies of our time. Developed by OpenAI, this extraordinary system is capable of generating astonishingly detailed images from textual descriptions. It pushes the boundaries of what we previously thought was achievable by machines, bridging the gap between our imagination and the digital canvas.

However, like any powerful tool, DALL-E must be wielded responsibly and ethically. The uncensored, limitless nature of its capabilities mandates the establishment of responsible usage guidelines. It is the collective responsibility of AI researchers, implementers, and users to ensure that DALL-E remains a force for positive growth and innovation while avoiding the pitfalls that come with wielding such potent technology.

Part 2: Responsible Usage Guidelines for DALL-E

Creating responsible usage guidelines for DALL-E is crucial to harness its immense power without encroaching upon ethical or societal boundaries. These guidelines offer a roadmap to ensure that the potential misuse of DALL-E is recognized and appropriately addressed. By adhering to these principles, we can foster an environment that encourages the creation of awe-inspiring art while maintaining respect for privacy, social values, and human autonomy.

1. Transparency and Accountability:

Understanding the inner workings of DALL-E is essential for responsible usage. AI researchers and implementers have a moral obligation to be transparent about the model's capabilities, limitations, and potential biases. Collaboration among experts should drive thorough evaluations and ethical training practices to address potential pitfalls that might arise from unintended biases or discriminatory outputs.

Furthermore, any application that uses DALL-E should keep a detailed record of the entire AI-assisted creative process, from input to output. This archive will allow for proper evaluation, scrutiny, and analysis of the ethical implications of the generated content.

2. Respect for Privacy:

Respecting privacy is key in the realm of AI and creative technology. Its deployment should be governed by strict data protection regulations, ensuring that the personal information of individuals remains confidential and secure. Prior informed consent should be obtained before using personal data to train, test, or improve DALL-E.

DALL-E's creators and users should be committed to preventing misuse that could lead to the unauthorized generation of images or infringe upon the privacy rights of individuals, communities, or organizations.

3. Ethical Rendering and Sensible Deployments:

The generated artwork using DALL-E holds immense power, and with it comes a great responsibility. Adhering to ethical standards is of utmost importance to prevent its usage for spreading misinformation, hate speech, or detrimental messages that can incite violence or discrimination.

AI-generated content should be subject to ethical review, both within organizations using DALL-E and by independent third parties accountable for maintaining just and harmonious societal values. Striking a balance between creative freedom and ethical compliance is the cornerstone for any legitimate deployment.

4. User Education and Regulation:

Promoting user education and public awareness is crucial to fostering responsible usage guidelines. Educating individuals about AI technology, its limitations, and implications will empower users to make informed decisions. It also enables them to appreciate the creative power while encouraging critical thinking and ethical analysis of the generated content.

Collaborative efforts by governments, academia, industry experts, and regulatory bodies should formulate policies and guidelines for the appropriate use of DALL-E. This will empower law enforcement agencies to address potential misuse or harmful deployment promptly.

Part 3: The Way Forward

Effective implementation of responsible usage guidelines for DALL-E demands a shared responsibility. Open dialogue among AI researchers, AI enthusiasts, policymakers, and the community at large is paramount in shaping the future of AI-assisted creativity.

Artificial intelligence and creative machines like DALL-E have the potential to revolutionize fields ranging from art and literature to advertising and marketing. With great power comes endless possibilities, but also the duty to exercise that power responsibly. Together, we can unlock the remarkable potential of this remarkable technology while keeping a steadfast hold on our ethical compass. Let us use DALL-E collaboratively, amplifying ideas, encouraging cohesion, and fostering an AI-human partnership worthy of our shared aspirations.

Chapter 9: Troubleshooting

Common Issues

DALL-E, a amalgamation of the name "Salvador Dali" and "Pixar's WALL-E," is a model capable of generating highly creative and unique images based on textual inputs provided by users. It combines principles from both image synthesis and language modeling to produce astonishing visual outputs. The beauty, complexity, and versatility of DALL-E captivate artists, designers, scientists, and curious minds across countless industries.

Section 2: Leveraging DALL-E for Common Issues

2. 1 Enhancing Creativity

One of the most captivating features of DALL-E is its ability to push the boundaries of human creativity. People often rely on DALL-E to generate inspiring and innovative images that can spark their own artistic ideas. By providing it with a set of parameters or textual constraints, such as "an ethereal landscape with floating islands and bioluminescent plants," DALL-E turns imagination into reality. Artists, graphic designers, and advertisers now find themselves empowered to overcome creative blocks and discover uncharted visual grounds.

2. 2 Solving Visual Design Challenges

In the realm of visual design, DALL-E emerges as a game-changer. Designers often need to create consistent, eye-catching visuals that resonate with their audience. However, this process can be laborious and time-consuming. DALL-E offers a fresh approach by allowing designers to quickly generate a multitude of designs, variations, or combinations based on the textual descriptions provided. Whether creating icons, logos, or infographics, designers can effortlessly receive a liason enabling them to promptly iterate, experiment, and refine their visual solutions.

2. 3 Facilitating Product Prototyping

Product prototyping is a critical stage for designers, engineers, and inventors. Creating physical prototypes can be costly and time-consuming. However, using DALL-E, one can visualize and conceptualize designs by equipping the model with specifications. For instance, engineers working on an autonomous vehicle can explain its functionality and desired aesthetics through textual descriptions. DALL-E translates those descriptions into photorealistic images, drastically accelerating the product development process. Thus, researchers and innovators can understand the precise aesthetics and features even before building a single physical prototype.

2. 4 Finding Inspiration for Fashion and Merchandise

DALL-E brings a wealth of creative possibilities to the world of fashion and merchandise. Fashion designers, stylists, and retailers often rely on visuals to inspire and captivate potential buyers. By leveraging DALL-E, they can articulate their ideas and designs, prompting DALL-E to generate high-resolution images resembling their vision of garments or products. This allows for swift exploration of various styles, cuts, materials, patterns, and color combinations without the need for physical prototypes. Consequently, a distinct blend of aesthetics and market preferences can be conveniently attained to generate successful product lines.

Section 3: Key Considerations and Ethical Guidelines

3. 1 Data Handling and Bias Mitigation

While DALL-E appears miraculous, practitioners must tread carefully to address inherent biases or inaccuracies. The underlying datasets for model training can unwittingly contain socio-cultural or demographic biases. It is critical to curate training sets that encompass diverse perspectives, cultures, and historical contexts. To ensure fairness and inclusivity, rigorous data audits must take place, and systematic efforts made to counter any form of discrimination in the training data. This serves the purpose of producing outputs that truly reflect societal richness and avoid reinforcing unjust stereotypes.

3. 2 Responsible Usage and Misinformation

Users must exercise ethical practices when using DALL-E to publish or distribute content. Misinformation, deceptive manipulations, and the spread of harmful narratives must be diligently avoided. Clear guidelines and best practices should govern the responsible use of DALL-E, ensuring transparency in leveraging its capabilities. By adhering to stringent ethical standards, society can harness the true potential of DALL-E to bring about positive change and address common issues.

As you embark on your journey to learn and employ DALL-E, keep in mind its transformative aptitude to fuel creativity, solve design challenges efficiently, facilitate product development, and guide fashion and merchandise choices. But always remember, with great power comes great responsibility.

Solutions and Workarounds

Beyond its evident artistic value, DALL-E holds incredible potential for solving complex problems by generating unique and innovative solutions. Whether you're an entrepreneur seeking fresh ideas, an engineer tackling technical challenges, or simply curious about the bounds of machine intelligence, DALL-E is poised to expand your creative horizons.

Part 2: Understand the Capabilities of DALL-E

To harness the potential of DALL-E, it is imperative to comprehend the foundations of its functioning and explore its boundaries. DALL-E operates by understanding textual prompts and transforming them into vivid, hyper-realistic images that hold a striking resemblance to the descriptions provided. From landscapes to fantastical creatures, DALL-E has been trained on an extensive dataset, enabling extraordinary diversity in its output.

It is crucial to note, however, that DALL-E does not possess an understanding of the objects and concepts it generates. It is a sophisticated generation tool that leverages patterns, correlations, and probabilistic modeling to deliver visually captivating outputs. As a result, DALL-E might occasionally conjure up surreal or even nonsensical images, reflecting the limitations of its underlying frameworks.

Part 3: Applications of DALL-E for Problem Solving

1. Ideation and Creativity Boost: DALL-E has the potential to become an indispensable tool for idea generation. It can assist entrepreneurs, artists, and designers in conceptualizing projects, generating fresh perspectives, and pushing creative boundaries.

2. Product Design and Visual Prototyping: DALL-E can expedite the design process by quickly rendering visual representations based on textual descriptions. It can aid in creating product mock-ups, architectural designs, or even fashion concepts.

3. Innovation and Invention: DALL-E's capacity to create complex and entirely novel objects opens the door to innovative businesses and inventions.

Combined with human input and ingenuity, DALL-E can provide technical insights and inspire new solutions to long-standing problems.

Part 4: Working Around DALL-E Limitations

While DALL-E undoubtedly provides a revolutionary toolset for ideation and problem-solving, it is essential to address its limitations and work around them effectively.

1. Use Clear and Specific Prompts: Clearly articulate your desired outcomes and provide precise prompts to guide DALL-E's image generation process. This reduces the likelihood of confusing or undesired results.

2. Iterative Collaboration: Engage in an iterative cycle of communication and feedback with DALL-E. Continuously refine and provide feedback on the generated images to prompt more accurate results aligned with your objectives.

3. Pre-filtering and Post-processing: Apply simple feature sets or visual constraints to narrow down DALL-E's imaginations. Post-process the generated images to filter out undesirable variations and refine them further.

Part 5: Ethical Considerations

As with any advanced technology, ethical considerations play a crucial role. DALL-E raises questions regarding copyright, data privacy, and the responsible use of AI-powered tools. When utilizing DALL-E, it is vital to respect legal and ethical boundaries, ensuring proper attribution and avoiding infringement.

Conclusion:

The rise of DALL-E has ushered in a new era of problem-solving and creativity. By leveraging its AI-powered generative abilities, individuals and teams can tap into its vast potential for envisioning fantastical ideas, tackling intricate engineering problems, and pushing the boundaries of innovation. Understanding DALL-E's capabilities, working around its limitations, and maintaining ethical considerations will undoubtedly enable users to harness its true power and change the game in problem-solving and solution generation.

Chapter 10: FAQs

Frequently Asked Questions

1\. What exactly is DALL-E.

DALL-E is a cutting-edge, generative adversarial network (GAN) developed by OpenAI, which uses deep learning algorithms to explore the power of image synthesis. Unlike traditional AI models with limited abilities, DALL-E can generate unique, novel images from textual descriptions, allowing users to witness the fusion of language and visual concepts. It performs image synthesis based on its ability to learn from vast amounts of data and extrapolates new content that aligns with human understanding, making it a remarkable feat in the field of AI.

2. How does DALL-E work.

DALL-E's operation is structured around a two-step process: pre-training and fine-tuning. During pre-training, the model is exposed to a broad range of internet text and corresponding images. It learns to predict the next word in a given sentence, thereby building on its language understanding capabilities. This process acquaints DALL-E with all sorts of semantic features, ensuring it possesses a vast knowledge base.

After pre-training, DALL-E moves into fine-tuning. OpenAI used a method known as score-based generative modeling to accomplish this. In fine-tuning, the model is trained on a highly curated dataset specifically designed for controlled generation. This dataset assists DALL-E in extracting visual prompts from textual input and translating them into coherent and visually appealing images, further enhancing its ability to generate content effectively.

3. Is DALL-E creative.

Yes, DALL-E can be considered truly creative. Rather than replicating existing images, it generates unique visuals based on textual instructions. By exploring constraints such as the angle, lighting, color, and unconventional shapes, DALL-E exhibits an elevated level of creativity. Its responses can evoke astonishment and awe due to its prowess in combining disparate ideas and generating striking visual representation.

4. Can DALL-E generate any image I describe.

While DALL-E is infused with a remarkable ability to produce unprecedented images, it does have certain limitations. At present, DALL-E has a cap on image resolution and struggles with detailed depictions. It tends to perform exceptionally well at composing novel images of everyday objects and animals, whereas rare or highly complex requests may be met with less accurate renderings. DALL-E is an evolving model, and researchers at OpenAI continue to devote ample resources to improving its capabilities.

5. How can DALL-E be beneficial in practical scenarios.

The utility of DALL-E stretches across various applications. Artists can leverage its creativity to generate unique visual concepts or supplemental images, breathing life into their creations. Advertisers can use this tool to design captivating illustrations tailored to specific messages, boosting engagement among customers. In the realm of transformative education, DALL-E can develop eye-catching presentations or generate vivid illustrations to aid understanding. Its potential extends to industries like fashion, gaming, and publishing, providing a plethora of possibilities for innovative storytelling.

Conclusion:

Housed within this chapter, we sought to answer some of the most commonly asked questions about DALL-E. We explored its intricate workings, its artistic flair, and its practical applications. By understanding the nuances of this exceptional amalgamation of AI and creativity, you are better equipped to unleash DALL-E's potential to revolutionize your own work in creative and insightful ways. So, let your imagination soar and embrace the ingenious nature of DALL-E.

Chapter 11: Resources

Additional Learning Materials

Section 1: Unleashing DALL-E's Creative Power

1. 1 Becoming an Idea Amplifier:

DALL-E possesses an immeasurable imaginative capacity to generate diverse and innovative ideas. It can be an invaluable aid for individuals seeking inspiration, particularly for developing additional learning materials. With DALL-E's help, your creativity knows no bounds.

1. 2 From Concepts to Visual Masterpieces:

One of DALL-E's most remarkable attributes is its ability to convert textual prompts into vivid and captivating images. We will unravel the magic behind DALL-E's processes, exploring how it learns and generates stunning visual creations. Witness the seamless blend of ingenuity and technology as ideas take shape on the canvas of pixel perfection.

Section 2: Leveraging DALL-E for Additional Learning Materials

2. 1 Innovative Visual Aids:

Tired of using plain and monotonous diagrams or images in your learning materials. DALL-E provides a delightful solution. Discover how AI-generated visuals can revolutionize the learning experience by capturing attention, enhancing comprehension, and leaving a lasting impression on the learners. Get ready to empower your materials with enticing infographics, engaging illustrations, and interactive diagrams tailored explicitly to your content.

2. 2 Educational Storytelling:

Imagine learning about historical events or scientific concepts through captivating visual narratives. Stories have always held a special place in our hearts, serving as powerful learning tools. DALL-E enables the creation of stunning storyboards, enabling educators and learners to embark on thrilling educational journeys through time, space, and knowledge. Brace yourself for an immersive and enthralling learning experience like never before.

2. 3 Enhancing Textbooks:

Traditional textbooks often fail to capture the desire and attention of modern learners. With DALL-E, our learning materials transcend the realms of monotony and embrace a new era of interactivity. By augmenting text-based content with visually rich illustrations, diagrams, and even 3D models, DALL-E empowers educators and learners to breathe life into seemingly arid topics. Witness how textbooks come alive, evoking the curiosity and wonderment necessary for effective learning.

Section 3: Ethical Considerations and Limitations

3. 1 Ethics of AI-Generated Visuals:

As we explore the immense potential of DALL-E for creating educational materials, it is essential to address ethical considerations. We shall navigate the boundaries of making AI-generated visuals ethically responsible, avoiding biases, and ensuring the content aligns with the educational objectives in an unbiased and inclusive manner. DALL-E encourages us to reflect on how AI can support rather than replace human creativity and expertise.

3. 2 Limitations and Overcoming Challenges:

Despite its impressive capabilities, DALL-E has inherent limitations. We will examine the challenges that may arise when using AI-generated materials, ranging from the constraints of dataset biases to the need for maintaining accuracy in educational context. This section will equip educators and content creators with strategies to maximize DALL-E's potential while mitigating any obstacles that might emerge.

Conclusion:

Among these exploration of DALL-E's world, we have witnessed the birth of digital Picasso, harnessed creativity unthinkable in isolation, and revolutionized the learning experience. The bridge between AI and education is only getting stronger. As we harness DALL-E's capabilities for generating additional learning material, let us embrace the synergy between human intellect and AI wizardry and envision a future where creativity continues to be amplified, and knowledge is effortlessly shared and celebrated by all.

Community Support

D ALL-E, a groundbreaking generative model developed by OpenAI, has revolutionized the field of artificial intelligence by merging the realms of language and visual creativity. Generating intricate images from text input, DALL-E has dazzled the world by its ability to create unparalleled visual representations of abstract concepts, whimsical ideas, and even surreal landscapes in an unparalleled blend of imagination and realism.

Amidst this chapter, we will explore how DALL-E can be harnessed to enhance and facilitate community support mechanisms. By leveraging the power of this AI model, community support initiatives can expand their reach, offer personalized advice, and empower individuals on their journeys towards personal growth and problem-solving.

Imagine a community support hotline that operates around the clock, bringing together volunteers from various backgrounds equipped with knowledge and experience on diverse topics. Together, they form a vast repository of expertise that can cater to the multifaceted issues faced by community members. Using DALL-E, an AI assistant could be set up to facilitate these conversations, offering support, understanding, and valuable recommendations to those in need.

The AI-powered assistant could read through messages, analyze their sentiment, identify key issues, and generate insightful responses aimed at providing genuine support. Drawing upon a vast database of community wisdom and carefully curated information, the assistant would use DALL-E's image generation capabilities to provide illustrative examples or visual aids, enhancing the quality and efficacy of guidance. For instance, when discussing home improvement, the AI assistant could generate images of potential remodels or furniture arrangements to help visualize options and facilitate decision-making.

Additionally, DALL-E could be employed to create visual representations of shared experiences to foster connection within a community. By generating art based on communal anecdotes or collective traits, individuals may feel a deeper sense of belonging and solidarity. For example, a poetry community could use DALL-E to illustrate a memorable line or theme from their works, highlighting shared poetic values and celebrating the beauty of creativity.

Going beyond verbal communication, DALL-E enables accessibility for individuals with disabilities who may require non-verbal means of expressing themselves. By encouraging users to describe their emotions, physical sensations, or environmental situations, the AI-powered assistant could generate lifelike images that bridge gaps in communication or provide a means to communicate without reliance on conventional channels.

When dealing with sensitive topics or emotional support, privacy and security become significant considerations in utilizing such advanced AI technology. Stricter regulations, ethical guidelines, and encrypted communication channels would need to be implemented to ensure privacy and protect the personal information shared during engagements with the AI assistant.

Furthermore, the seamless collaboration between humans and AI could facilitate peer support initiatives within communities. Passionate experts could work alongside the AI assistant, using DALL-E as a tool to create engaging content, educational material, or motivational artworks to uplift and stimulate community members, thereby fostering mutual growth and collective empowerment.

As DALL-E continues to evolve and improve, it has the potential to become an invaluable asset to community support networks, expanding the avenues for inclusion, compassion, and progress. By leveraging this innovative AI model, communities can transform the way individuals interact, receive guidance, and navigate life's challenges, making community support accessible to all.

Chapter 12: Case Studies

Real-life Examples

U nlike any previous model, DALL-E was not restricted to mundane objects or conventional art. It had the peculiarity of being able to generate images based on text prompts, turning ordinary words into astonishing pictures. The scale of DALL-E's abilities exceeded our wildest imagination, enabling access to an endless array of visual possibilities. The days of painstakingly crafting visions by hand were over - endless inspiration now lay only a few prompts away.

Aspiring artists flocked to DALL-E, eagerly experimenting with its seemingly boundless capabilities. The talented painter, Anna, could invoke evocative scenes onto her canvas just by describing them succinctly. Similarly, Eric, a budding comic book artist, could conjure full-color panels depicting epic battles between heroes by summarizing a few sentences. Creating unique imagery became an enthralling and accessible endeavor, limited only by the depths of one's imagination.

Inspired by such tales of AI-generated artistry, organizations embraced DALL-E as a groundbreaking tool for design and marketing campaigns. Brand strategists, advertising agents, and logo designers eagerly tapped into DALL-E's vast repertoire, seeking visual marvels specifically tailored to their needs. Crafting logos or product visuals that projected brands' visions turned into a fluid process, with DALL-E at the helm, amalgamating imagination and technical prowess.

Within the architectural realm, DALL-E sparked a revolution—a utopia realized at the mere mention of specific architecture elements and themes—balancing the dreams of esteemed architects with real-world constraints. Blueprint sketches transformed into breathtaking renderings of exotic cityscapes, sustainable housing solutions emerged spontaneously from simple descriptions, and grandiose structures appeared on paper within moments. The fusion of urban planning and avant-garde design became both feasible and spectacular—an architectural renaissance forged through the symbiotic relationship between AI and human creativity.

Mysteries unraveling within the entertainment industry were no longer obscured in the folds of imagination or complex storyboards. Writers, directors, and producers could plot their plots by conjuring vibrant and awe-inspiring movie scenes mediated by DALL-E's genius. Special effects supervisors marveled at the ease with which mythical beasts and majestic landscapes could be brought to life. The beauty of DALL-E's implementation was that its hyper-realistic generation bridged the gap between abstract concepts and tangible results - materializing dreams thought impossible.

As remarkable as DALL-E is, it did not confine itself to creative endeavors alone. Scientists, too, were lured by its enigmatic potential—gaining access to the enclaves of the universe's mysteries through the prism of AI. Astrophysics stepped into an era of visualization unparalleled. By describing distant celestial objects or hypothetical scenarios, physicists could present their far-ranging ideas and prospects without numerical scribbles or elaborate equations. Discovery radiated in colors unseen, as breakthroughs veiled in imagination emerged in vivid hues and clear contours.

In the coming years, DALL-E took not only art but various scientific fields to unprecedented heights. It shattered the limitations imposed by static imagery. Newfound perspectives collided with the ethereal, transforming orthodox thoughts into tangible reality—a cosmic ripple that vowed to redefine our comprehension of creativity, enabling the world to weave together the realms of imagination and data-driven precision with ease.

Human curiosity, propelled by DALL-E, flourished. No longer confined to predetermined realities, boundaries of our imagination began to fade away, gradually merging with AI-imbued creativity. The tangible results of that unimaginable fusion fostered systemic change—ushering in an era transcending human cognition's traditional bounds, where the beauty of tangible dreams unravelled even our most cherished concepts of possibility.

Success Stories

1. DALL-E and Graphic Design:

The art of graphic design has witnessed a momentous shift with the integration of DALL-E. Its ability to generate highly intricate and aesthetically pleasing images has equipped designers with an unprecedented arsenal of resources. Needless to say, DALL-E empowers graphic designers to expand their creative boundaries and brings novel approaches to project fruition. Whether it be creating captivating visual branding elements or designing unique customer experiences within digital platforms, DALL-E has proved its worth by saving countless hours spent on manual design iterations, thus enhancing productivity and cost-effectiveness.

2. DALL-E and Fashion Industry:

Fashion, renowned for its ever-evolving trends and ceaseless experimentation, has found an indomitable ally in DALL-E. By inputting textual descriptions of desired clothing articles or design cues, DALL-E readily translates the vision into visually striking illustrations. Leading fashion designers cue into DALL-E's ability to construct avant-garde clothing concepts, saving precious time in the ideation phase. With designers applying these illustrative representations in their sketches or digital renderings, DALL-E facilitates quicker prototyping and pushes the envelope of fashion design, combining innovation and creativity in ways never before imagined.

3. DALL-E and Architecture:

Architecture, a realm where creativity harmonizes with precision, has witnessed game-changing possibilities through DALL-E's interventions. Presenting architects with the ability to bring ethereal concepts into virtual reality, DALL-E enables a remarkable visualization of spatial designs with detailed illustrations of exterior facades, artistic interventions, or customized interior layouts. By capturing design philosophies diligently recorded through concise textual descriptions, architects effortlessly collaborate with consultants, developing ideas with unprecedented efficiency. As a result, complexities and discrepancies in conceptualizations significantly reduce, allowing for smoother project execution, enhanced collaboration, and improved client communication.

4. DALL-E and Marketing:

For marketing professionals, DALL-E provides an indispensable advantage in developing unique visual campaigns and creating eye-catching content. With just a text prompt, marketers can spark the generation of stunning visual assets for advertising, branding, and content marketing purposes. The generation time is significantly reduced, allowing marketers to promptly validate ideas and explore diverse possibilities. By leveraging DALL-E within marketing campaigns, brands stand out among competitors and effortlessly capture consumers' attention with unmatched visual impact.

Conclusion:

The success stories surrounding DALL-E serve as inspiring evidence of its transformative capabilities and multitude of applications. With a focus on enhancing creative endeavors, DALL-E has proven itself as a vital tool in fields ranging from graphic design to architecture, fashion, and marketing. Its ability to bring textual descriptions to life with stunning visualizations pushes the boundaries of what is possible, unlocking new levels of creativity and efficiency in various industries. As DALL-E continues to evolve and democratize access to creative resources, its impact is poised to revolutionize how we approach innovation and shape the possibilities that lie ahead.

Chapter 13: Future Outlook

DALL-E's Future Developments

Navigating the terrain of DALL-E's future developments presents an exciting glimpse into the potential advancements on the horizon. One avenue that researchers are exploring is expanding DALL-E's training dataset to encompass an even broader range of concepts, giving rise to an even more nuanced understanding of the world. Efforts are being made to incorporate more diverse subjects, cultures, and historical references to refine DALL-E's knowledge base and foster more contextually appropriate image generation.

Another facet of DALL-E's future lies in elevating its imaginative capabilities to new heights. While DALL-E can create impressive visuals based on the given prompts, there is room for growth in its ability to effortlessly generate realistic and intricate details. Researchers have set their sights on enhancing DALL-E's adeptness at synthesizing complex objects, dynamic scenes, and displaying a deeper understanding of lighting, shadows, and perspective.

Concurrently, work is being done to refine the interactive functionality of DALL-E. As of now, users can only specify a single textual prompt to generate an image. However, researchers envision expanding this capability to incorporate multi-prompt support, allowing users to capture intricate and layered visual compositions in a single image generation process. This advancement will enable creative professionals to express their vision with much greater precision and artistic control.

Amidst these advancements, researchers are also exploring the ethical implications tied to the usage and impact of DALL-E. As this immensely powerful AI model gains popularity, discussions surrounding copyright, intellectual property, and attribution have come to the forefront. Addressing these concerns is crucial to establishing a balance between fostering creativity and respecting the originality of human creators.

Furthermore, the potential integration of DALL-E into real-world applications holds promise for various industries. Architectural firms can envision buildings and interiors before construction commences, fashion designers can showcase avant-garde designs without physically producing them, and filmmakers can visualize scenes and special effects with remarkable ease. These potential applications pave the way for a new wave of innovation and efficiency.

In conclusion, DALL-E's future holds immense possibilities, fueled by the passion and ingenuity of researchers and developers seeking to push the boundaries of creativity and AI. As the model continues to mature, it will undoubtedly shape how we visualize and interact with the world. With each new development and refinement, DALL-E is poised to redefine art, design, and the very nature of imagination. The journey ahead is exhilarating, heralding a future where the power of AI interweaves seamlessly with human creativity.

Emerging Trends in AI Art

Chapter 14: Conclusion

Summary of Key Points

DALL-E, named after the celebrated artist Salvador Dalí and the character Wall-E from Pixar's animated film, represents a revolutionary deep learning model created by OpenAI, an artificial intelligence laboratory prioritizing the development of advanced AI technologies for the betterment of society. It is specifically designed to generate highly realistic images from textual descriptions, bridging the gap between language and visual representation in an unprecedented manner.

Delving deeper into the essence of DALL-E, it utilizes an innovative implementation of the GPT-3 architecture (another phenomenal AI model developed by OpenAI). GPT-3, short for "Generative Pre-trained Transformer 3," triggered a paradigm shift in natural language processing tasks by constructing predictive models based on textual inputs. DALL-E, riding on the success of GPT-3, extends this capability to the domain of images - finally allowing for the creation of coherent, vivid images from a textual prompt.

The training process of DALL-E involves utilizing a meticulously curated dataset comprising over 12 billion image-text pairs. This extensive dataset serves as a rich source of deep learning that allows DALL-E to grasp semantic relationships between concepts, contextual nuances, and visual patterns. Such comprehensive training transcends the capabilities of previous image generation models, giving rise to remarkably novel possibilities within the field of computer vision.

One of the most extraordinary aspects of DALL-E is its ability to interpret and understand sometimes ambiguous and abstract textual prompts to generate coherent images. For instance, when prompted with the words "an armchair in the shape of an avocado," DALL-E would produce an impressively detailed and photo-realistic visual representation of this imaginative fusion. The impressive accuracy and attention to detail showcased by DALL-E expedite the creative workflow for visual artists and designers, while also promising enhanced accessibility and inclusivity in various industries.

OpenAI formally introduced DALL-E to the world with a myriad of jaw-dropping examples that left experts and the public in awe of its untapped potential. People marveled at the unique, fantastical creatures brought to life by DALL-E, generated solely from textual descriptions. Whether it is a fire-breathing dragon with the head of a snow leopard, traversing through a moonlit forest, or a teapot in the shape of a hot air balloon sailing amidst a sunset sky, DALL-E's prowess exceeds expectations at every turn.

Understanding the transformative power of DALL-E, militarized organizations also recognized its potential in unparalleled ways. The ability to generate realistic images seamlessly based on specific textual descriptions presents a range of awe-inspiring military applications, such as creating accurate simulations for tactical training or generating visually realistic threats in military strategic simulations.

However, with its incredible capabilities come considerable ethical considerations. The generation of lifelike, high-resolution content potentially ushers in a new era of misinformation. As DALL-E empowers anyone, regardless of technical know-how, to create plausible yet fabricated visual content, previously reliable forms of media and sources can become increasingly susceptible to abuse. OpenAI, responsible for birthing DALL-E, is fully aware of these ethical quandaries and actively considers the implications and ways to mitigate associated risks.

In conclusion, DALL-E represents an exciting frontier of artificial intelligence, revolutionizing image generation by converging textual descriptions and visual representation with astonishing precision. Its ability to create vivid, realistic images from nothing but textual prompts unlocks a plethora of unprecedented possibilities across diverse industries. However, these innovations also demand contemplation of the ethical implications and a proactive approach to address potential challenges as this breakthrough technology unfolds further. The future of DALL-E promises limitless imagination and transformative potential, effectively blurring the lines between creativity, imagination, and artificial intelligence.

Final Thoughts

A t its core, DALL-E is a uniquely trained neural network that combines features of both Convolutional Neural Networks (CNNs) and Transformers, making it capable of generating high-quality, coherent, and detailed images from textual descriptions. By utilizing a multi-headed attention mechanism, DALL-E is able to leverage global context and generate nuanced details, resulting in images that often appear strikingly realistic or bizarrely surreal, depending on the given prompt.

The training process for DALL-E involved exposing it to a vast dataset consisting of text-image pairs, expertly curated by the OpenAI team. The dataset encompassed a wide range of visual elements and concepts, presenting DALL-E with a rich tapestry of information to learn from. By repeatedly fine-tuning its parameters through millions of iterations, DALL-E gradually developed an ability to understand relationships between various objects, textures, and arrangements, ultimately enabling it to synthesize original images.

The potential uses and applications of DALL-E are vast and varied, extending beyond the realm of artistic creativity. Its impact on industries such as advertising, design, and entertainment is potentially transformative. With DALL-E, designers and marketers can now effortlessly browse and select from a seemingly endless repertoire of compelling, AI-generated visual designs, streamlining creative processes and pushing the boundaries of visual aesthetics.

Moreover, DALL-E holds tremendous promise in domains like architecture and urban planning. Architects could describe their concepts in great detail, and DALL-E would produce photorealistic images, assisting in visualizing unconventional designs or exploring new possibilities. City planners could employ DALL-E to envision future landscapes, visualizing concepts like efficiently designed public spaces or eco-friendly infrastructure, thereby facilitating more informed decision-making.

Outside the professional realm, DALL-E empowers individuals to explore the depths of their imagination, collaboratively creating and enhancing artwork.

Artists can now unleash their creativity onto a digital canvas, sparking a rich symbiotic dance between human vision and AI ingenuity. This marriage between human expression and AI augmentation presents new opportunities for artistic expression and promotes a democratization of creative talent.

However, like any powerful technology, the nuances of DALL-E and AI-generated creativity come with a set of responsible considerations. As we admire and find fascination in the capabilities of DALL-E, we must also acknowledge the ethical responsibilities accompanying this revolutionary tool. Ensuring that AI-generated visuals are used judiciously, respecting intellectual property, cultural sensitivities, and privacy concerns, is paramount in nurturing the rightful integration of AI into our daily lives.

In conclusion, DALL-E marks a pivotal milestone in the ongoing evolution of artificial intelligence. Its ability to confidently generate complex and visually coherent images in response to textual prompts introduces unprecedented possibilities across a multitude of industries. As we venture further into this burgeoning era of AI-enhanced creativity, it is essential to embrace the potential that DALL-E and similar innovative models offer, while simultaneously keeping ethical considerations at the forefront of our minds, fostering a more profound partnership between human ingenuity and artificial intelligence.

Chapter 15: Glossary

Key Terms and Definitions

Section 1: Understanding DALL-E's Origin and Design

1. 1 A Ray of Light in the Deep Learning Era

In recent years, deep learning has witnessed tremendous progress in the realm of language and image processing. Generative models have emerged as a popular avenue, enabling the creation of novel content using the power of artificial intelligence. Among them, DALL-E is a prime example of the strides made in bridging the traditional (and seemingly unrelated) fields of linguistics and visual arts.

1. 2 The Birth of DALL-E

DALL-E, a name crafted from a fusion of iconic paintings by Salvador Dalí and the popular internet meme tradition, embraces a dual character that exemplifies its essence. Conceived by a team of OpenAI researchers, DALL-E represents the amalgamation of state-of-the-art machine learning algorithms, computationally intensive training procedures, and creative ingenuity.

Section 2: Unraveling the Inner Workings of DALL-E

2. 1 THE POWER OF TRANSFORMERS: Initializing the Unsealed Universe

Transformers, a variant of deep neural networks driven by attention mechanisms, act as the backbone of DALL-E's computational framework. This paradigm shift from traditional convolutional architectures not only enhances the model's processing speed but also enables it to capture intricate long-range dependencies within textual and visual inputs.

2. 2 Encoding Descriptions: Breathing Life Into Pixels

To augment images from textual descriptions, DALL-E relies on an encoding process that effectively captures salient features and the good splines of language. By transforming words into numeric representations using word embeddings and positional encodings, DALL-E infuses linguistic context into its generative process.

2. 3 Creative Co-Traversal of the Latent Space: Discovering New Dimensions

One of the most astonishing aspects of DALL-E lies in its ability to traverse a vast latent space comprised of z-vectors - condensed representations of abstract concepts. This capability grants DALL-E the unprecedented talent to generate images that represent controlled transformations of the latent variables, allowing exploration of novel, uncharted visual spaces.

Section 3: Nurturing Your DALL-E Education

3. 1 HARNESSING THE Power of Key Terms and Definitions

To effectively learn and use DALL-E, one must first familiarize themselves with specific key terms and definitions essential to comprehending its remarkable capabilities. This book serves as an innovative guide, highlighting imperative concepts and elucidating the theoretical underpinnings of DALL-E to unlock its full potential.

3. 2 Implications and Limitations

As DALL-E gleams on the horizon of technological advancements, humankind must confront the ramifications and limitations arising from its existence. Concerns about bias, potential misuse, and the blurred lines between AI-created content and human-generated work demand our attention for responsible adoption and development.

Conclusion

In the following chapters, we will embark on a journey of discovery, unraveling the limitless possibilities awaiting those who venture into the world of DALL-E. Exploring various applications and inspiring examples, we will witness how this AI breakthrough reshapes our creative landscape by blending art and algorithms in ways never thought possible. Ready your imagination; DALL-E is set to challenge the boundaries of creativity and propel us into a futuristic realm filled with AI-generated masterpieces.

Milton Keynes UK
Ingram Content Group UK Ltd.
UKHW022041290324
440241UK00015B/639